Don't Say "$#%&X" in Church!

What if one prayer
could change your view
of God and money?

Bo Chancey

Don't Say "$#%&X" in Church!
Published by 41Press

© 2015 by Bo Chancey

1 3 5 7 9 10 8 6 4 2

For information or bulk sales:
41PRESS
7200 Queens Place
Amarillo, TX 79109

publisher@41press.com

ISBN: 978-0-9968757-0-7

Contents

The Agenda

Let's talk about money and God. More directly...let's talk about your money and your God.

That probably set off some alarms. Right now sirens are blaring, spotlights are glaring, and your mind is searching the perimeter for potential breaches. We are generally okay with having conversations about money or conversations about God, but conversations about our money and our God are off-limits. It is okay to discuss God in general and money in general, but let's not make this personal. When the God-money topic is addressed in a personal fashion, most people go into some version of full lockdown mode.

I am hopeful that we can find a way to drop the defenses and get to the heart of the matter because the God-money topic is always a heart matter. If you are still reading, we are on the right track. You made it all the way to paragraph three and the book is still in hand. This is good. We can work with this.

It is okay to be skeptical, cynical and guarded. I get that, and I cannot say that I blame you.

We live in a manipulative world. People lie and misrepresent to get what they want. Christianity is not immune to this perversion. Abuses of money are as old as the Church.

Judas had a money issue. He was a thief who helped himself to the money that was provided for Jesus and the disciples (John 12:6). Ananias and Sapphira lied about a donation they made to the Church, and they died on the spot (Acts 5). The church in Corinth had an issue with lawsuits among believers (1 Corinthians 6). As you move through church history, you find all kinds of abuses: the crusades, selling indulgences, bribery, taxation, oppression of the poor, and false doctrines like the prosperity-give-to-get health-and-wealth preaching that is prevalent today.

So here we are with an important heart issue that sparks a wide-range of negative emotion at the mere hint of the topic being brought up. This is precisely why I have no intention of hinting at it or beating around the bush. There will be no back door approach, no bait and switch, no smoke and mirrors and the like. It seems to me like we have had plenty of that nonsense and we need a simple no-nonsense approach.

I picked up a book on biblical stewardship recently and the opening paragraph made the bold claim that the author had no agenda in writing the book. This seemed absurd to me. Why write a book if you have no agenda? Furthermore, why read a book if it was written without an agenda? I assume that the author was trying to ease fears by attempting to communicate that he had no hidden agenda, but even that struck me as disingenuous and a bit manipulative.

Look, this book has an agenda. My primary purpose is not to provide false comfort to your very real fears. Money can be a scary thing. When we do not handle money in the way God desires, money starts to handle us. Money dominates our thinking, controls our decisions, impacts our emotions and sets the tone for our relationships. Money becomes our god, and money makes a terrible god.

So, yes, this book has an agenda. This is first and foremost a lordship book. Is Jesus your Lord or not? He was crystal clear on this issue when He said, "You cannot serve both God and money" (Matthew 6:24). People have tried to use God to serve money, and awful abuses have ensued. Conversely, people have used money to serve God, and beautiful blessings have been bestowed.

Consider the charity work done in the name of Jesus through His Church. Think of the billions of people the Church has helped by the generosity unleashed through handling money in ways God desires. We have hospitals, homeless shelters, orphanages, addiction programs, mental health care, mission agencies, adoption agencies, prison ministries and so much more. It is impossible to imagine how dark our world would be if not for the light of God shining through the generosity of His Church.

But there is so much more we are called to do and we need to know it depends on us to get it done.

I have an agenda. I want you to demonstrate your trust in God by giving money generously to Him through your local church.

Wait!

Before you throw this book across the room and attempt to forget what you have already read, I dare you to do one thing. That's right.

I am calling you out. I dare you to pray a bold prayer. What could it hurt?

Pray this prayer: "God, show me what percentage of my income is generous."

Everyone gives a percentage of their income to God...it ranges between 0%-100%. You are already giving a percentage, but do you know what it is and whether it is generous? Ask God to show you what He desires.

This prayer is the foundation for the remainder of this book. Every time you are tempted to go into lockdown mode, just stop and pray, "God show me what percentage of my income is generous."

chapter one

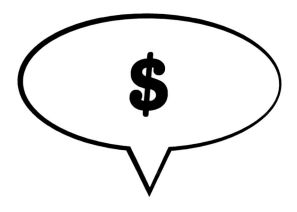

MONEY matters. It matters to you and it matters to God.

It matters to your family and friends.

People care about money. It can dominate our thoughts, conversations and dreams. We plan our days around money...jobs to acquire money, errands to spend money and efforts to save money. We are saddened over lost money and excited over found money. Our emotions are often tied to money or consuming things provided by money. Money can directly impact happiness, fear, anxiety, satisfaction, peace of mind and just about every other emotion on the spectrum.

Lives are spent on a cyclical pattern of earn, consume, throw away, repeat. It is easy to get lost while navigating the pitfalls of a consumer-driven culture. Temporary things become ultimate things. Lifestyle maintenance and building can easily supersede pursuits that lead to lasting soul satisfaction. Without realizing it, we are carried away by the cultural tide and set adrift in the sea of consumerism. Almost everyone drowns.

We drown in debt. We drown in overconsumption. We drown in the folly of self-sufficiency and vain indulgence. We struggle and grasp at things to save us, but eventually we are pulled under, as the consumers become the consumed.

But money is not the problem. Money is neither good nor evil. It is simply a thing for us to use. Our grand mistake is that we reverse roles with money and the spenders are spent. Lives are spent in the pursuit of more, but more is never enough. We consume, work, struggle and save, but what happens in the end?

We all die and today's treasure becomes tomorrow's trash.

My grandmother lived to be 99 years old. Her longevity allowed me to witness a gradual downsizing as opposed to a more typical sudden end. In her mid-nineties we moved her from her home on a lake to a one-bedroom apartment in an assisted living center. My Dad and I loaded a truck with her furniture, clothes, pictures, appliances, and so forth to set her up in her new home. As her health deteriorated, she was moved to different units in order to provide better care for her. Each move meant less stuff.

When she died, I went with my Dad to clear out her room. I made note of what was left. Ninety-nine years came down to three boxes of pictures, a dresser, a nightstand, a chair, a lamp, two bags of clothes, and a bag of trash.

I shared this observation with my Dad, and he smiled and said, "Isn't that great?"

Yes. It is great. I am thankful that I got to have this hands-on lesson on life and death. In the end, stuff did not matter because her true identity had nothing to do with where she lived or what she owned. The focus of her funeral was all about relationships. She was known as daughter, sister, friend, wife, mother, grandmother, great-grandmother, aunt, teacher, church-member and most importantly, child of God.

We would all do well to remember that our baseline identity is child of God. We are created by God to be in a relationship with God. He invites us into His eternal family, and life is meant to be about knowing Him and making Him known. Money is a part of the world we live in and in order to navigate this life effectively, we must put money in it its proper place by using it wisely. If we fail to intentionally use money, money will end up using us. It can easily become an obsession that dominates our thoughts, motivations and efforts.

Our clichés regarding money are telling. "Money doesn't grow on trees." "Money makes the world go 'round." "Time is money." "Another day, another dollar." We are a money-obsessed culture.

This is nothing new. The pursuit of wealth and the power that comes with it is evident throughout human history. We are not the first people to put our trust, hope, and faith in an economic system and we certainly will not be the last.

God understands that money matters to us, and since it matters to us, it matters to Him. He provides direction for how we are to handle money so that money does not handle us. The Bible contains over 2,000 verses about money. Jesus used money more than any other subject in His teachings. Almost half of the parables and 15% of Jesus' teachings are centered on money. God provides us with His vast instructions on money because He knows how much we struggle with it.

Since God speaks about how money impacts our relationships with Him, we too should speak on this topic. It is foolish to ignore the God-money conversation. God wants us to engage in this controversial topic and seek His wisdom for how to navigate the world we live in. Ignoring God's wisdom on money makes us ignorant, and out of our ignorance we say ignorant things.

Believe me, as a preacher, I have heard and said some pretty foolish things regarding money in church. Let's go ahead and deal with the top five reactions people express when the church and God start to meddle in their financial affairs.

1. "Every time I go to church, all they talk about is money."

If that is true, then maybe God is trying to tell you something. If you only attend worship services a few times a year, and each time you go the subject matter is money, I would propose it is not a coincidence. I encourage you to pay attention and keep going. Sometimes God has a message for us that we want to reject, but He insists on teaching us because He knows we cannot move forward until we understand.

Most churches avoid speaking about money like the plague. They relegate the topic to one brief series a year and an occasional one-off sermon to reinforce the overall message.

Preachers are like everyone else…they want to be liked, they want to be listened to, and they generally do not enjoy making people uncomfortable. Preaching on money is difficult and creates a delicate tension, but it is absolutely essential to biblical preaching. Jesus utilized money in His teachings 15% of the time. If His Church follows His pattern, then we should be preaching on money about eight times a year.

That is probably about seven-and-a-half times more often than anyone would like, but the Church is not in the catering business. We are in the seeking-and-saving-the-lost business and the stakes are high. Comfort is not our mission. Jesus came to set the captives free, not to make the prison plush. The love of money holds hordes of people in captivity. The good news of the gospel delivers us from the bondage of greed and releases us to lead others to freedom. Even if money has no hold on your heart, I guarantee that you know numerous people who are held hostage by it. God speaks through His Church and He may be preparing you to help someone else.

So, if every time you go to church all they talk about is money…pay attention.

2. "My money is my personal business and has nothing to do with my relationship with God."

Anytime we compartmentalize our relationships with God, we create problems.

Lordship is all encompassing. We cannot make certain things off-limits to the lordship of Christ. Doing so divides the heart and leads to all manner of sin.

If you are a Christian, then it is no longer your money; it is God's money. This is the basic truth of stewardship. The struggle over generous giving is impossible to overcome until this basic principle is accepted. Jesus is Lord. Everything is His. We are His stewards. He allows us to manage His money. Whatever money is entrusted to us belongs to God, and we must all give an account for how we use it. This massive shift in thinking changes everything. We are God's money managers and should never think in terms of "my money."

God cares about how we use His money. Our bank accounts tell stories. What kind of story does your bank account tell? Is it a story of generosity, faith, and trust, or does it tell a different story?

God cares about how we use His money, and He pays attention to our giving. Does this upset you? Are you repulsed by the thought of God caring about money? Are you concerned about what He sees?

The fact that God is watching does not need to produce negative emotions. Instead, it could produce great joy. I have a friend who once told me about how he reminds his children that God is watching them. My initial response to him was one of shock and concern. I explained to him that I felt like that statement promoted an inappropriate view of God…like an angry God in the sky just waiting to zap devious little boys and girls with lightning bolts of wrath. My friend simply shook his head and explained that he does not tell his children that God is watching when they do wrong things; he reminds them that God is watching when they do good things.

Light bulb!

God is watching. He is watching when we do what He wants and He feels great pleasure in the faithful actions of His children. Does God delight in how you utilize His money?

Consider the story of the widow's offering.

"Jesus sat down opposite the place where the offerings were put and watched the crowd putting their money into the temple treasury. Many rich people threw in large amounts. But

a poor widow came and put in two very small copper coins, worth only a few cents.

Calling his disciples to him, Jesus said, 'Truly I tell you, this poor widow has put more into the treasury than all the others. They all gave out of their wealth; but she, out of her poverty, put in everything—all she had to live on.'"

Mark 12:41-44

Jesus watched what people gave. The generosity of the widow's offering was noteworthy, and Jesus pointed it out to His disciples. He compared her offering to the offerings of others and He declared that hers was the greatest. Jesus revealed that she put in everything—all she had to live on. The widow held nothing back from God. She had no money because it was all God's money. This realization is where authentic lordship begins. A proper view of money is required to faithfully follow Jesus.

God is watching. Is that good or bad news?

Many people believe that giving is a private matter between only the individual and God. This is an unfortunate untruth that damages the work God longs to do through His Church. The hyper-application of a misinterpretation of one statement by Jesus has reinforced the faulty notion that giving is strictly a private matter.

You may already have the scripture in mind.

"So when you give to the needy, do not announce it with trumpets, as the hypocrites do in the synagogues and on the streets, to be honored by others. Truly I tell you, they have received their reward in full. But when you give to the needy, do not let your left hand know what your right hand is doing, so that your giving may be in secret. Then your Father, who sees what is done in secret, will reward you."
Matthew 6:2-4

This is a heart issue. First of all, it does merit pointing out that Jesus said "when" you give not "if" you give. Giving is assumed. Secondly, Jesus is referring to efforts to use giving for personal advancement. If you give so that others will think more highly of you, to make a name for yourself, to gain a position of power, and so forth, then you are not giving to glorify God. In essence, you are not really giving. Instead, you are spending money to get something for yourself. Whatever you acquire is your reward. When we give to God, He is glorified and His name is remembered. The reward is that we are sharing in our Father's business.

Giving is always a heart issue. Jesus' statement has far more to do with the heart behind giving than with the methodology of giving. Obviously, we are not to toot our own horns in giving, but we overstep the scriptures when we relegate giving to being nobody's business but our own.

Giving is a communal matter. It matters to God, it matters to the individual, it matters to the Church, and it matters to world we live in. God is glorified through the generosity of His Church.

Consider these scriptures from the New Testament that demonstrate that giving was not kept private.

- The Widow's Offering (Mark 12:41-44 & Luke 21:1-4)
- Mary anointed Jesus with expensive perfume. (John 12:1-8)
- Zacchaeus stood up and declared that he would give half his possessions to the poor. (Luke 19:1-8)

- Barnabas was acknowledged for selling a field and giving the money to the Church. (Acts 4:36-37)
- Ananias and Sapphira's gift and lying about the gift were public matters. (Acts 5:1-11)
- Tabitha's generosity was recognized. (Acts 9:36)
- Cornelius was known for his generosity. (Acts 10:1-2)
- Pheobe was acknowledged as being a benefactor of many people. (Romans 16:1-2)
- Paul wrote that Stephanas, Fortunatus, and Achaicus deserved recognition for their generosity. (1 Corinthians 16:15-18)
- The Macedonian churches were used as an example of generosity. (2 Corinthians 8:1-2)
- We are told to test the sincerity of our love by comparing it with the earnestness of others in regards to giving. (2 Corinthians 8:8-11)
- The book of Philippians is in large part a thank you letter from Paul to the Philippian church for their generosity.

Why does this matter?

It matters because giving is difficult and people need to be encouraged to give. Testimonies about the joy of giving encourage others to give. Recognizing generosity provides examples of giving leaders to follow and emulate. Expressing thanks to those who give is important for the mutual encouragement of everyone involved.

Giving for the purpose of being thanked or recognized is wrong, but it is also wrong not to recognize and thank givers. The truly humble can simply say, "You are welcome" when they are thanked for being generous to the Lord and allow their generosity to be an encouragement to others to give.

3. "Churches are so greedy. All they want is my money."

Christ-centered churches want more people in the kingdom of heaven. If churches are greedy for anything, it ought to be for lost people being found. Money is simply a tool used for seeking and saving the lost.

There is a financial cost associated with achieving the mission of Christ. A direct correlation exists between the resources given to a local congregation and the scope of ministry the church is able to provide. Facilities, staff members and programs cost money. Churches depend on the generosity of their people to meet financial obligations and propel the mission of the church.

What churches really want is your heart. When your heart is invested in the kingdom-building work of Jesus, you become passionately consumed with matters of eternal significance. Churches engage people at the heart level to enlist them into God's family business.

> *"For where your treasure is, there your heart will be also."*
> **Luke 12:34**

Jesus said that people's hearts follow their money. Churches know the value of investing in eternity and must communicate an unpopular message. Jesus wants your life to matter. He longs to use you to build His eternal kingdom. Giving is a tangible way to pursue the mission of Jesus. It sets hearts on a path toward Jesus and His mission.

Do churches want you to give money? Yes.

Is money all churches want? No.

Money is merely a means to an end, but it matters. Give and your heart will follow. Give and there will be more people in the kingdom of heaven. Give and you will invest in eternity.

Give.

Now if this seems a bit heavy-handed and your repulsion is growing…do not disengage. The discomfort is normal. I probably should have warned you that you would feel a little pressure. This is a bit like going to the doctor for a check-up. The doctor is going to poke and prod to find sensitive areas. Sensitivity is often a sign that there is a problem.

If you feel ouchy in regards to money, I implore you to pay attention to those symptoms. Feelings like anger, fear, worry, agitation, irritation and shame are symptoms of a deeper issue…a heart issue…a lordship issue. There is a remedy. It is called giving. Take your medicine and give. Your heart will follow your money, and those irritating symptoms will be replaced with things like love, joy, peace, patience, kindness, goodness, faithfulness, gentleness, and self-control.

4. "I feel so guilty. I'll throw all the cash I have on me into the offering today in an attempt to appease God."

Guilt is not from God.

Godly sorrow, on the other hand, is something entirely different.

> *"Godly sorrow brings repentance that leads to salvation and leaves no regret, but worldly sorrow brings death."*
> **2 Corinthians 7:10**

God is done with guilt offerings. Jesus took care of that on the cross. Giving to God out of guilt will do nothing to change your heart. Guilt is different from godly sorrow. Guilt is defeat. Godly sorrow is victory. Guilt focuses on sin. Godly sorrow focuses on the good we ought to do. Guilt sucks you under in a rip current of shame. Godly sorrow lifts you up to set you free.

Godly sorrow leads to repentance. Repentance is a change in mindset. Guilt might produce a one-time reaction, but godly sorrow leads to world-view transformation. Repentance sets the stage for perpetual growth.

Guilt allows you to feel exactly the same way about money as you did before. It puts the focus on you and can actually make greed grow. Godly sorrow changes you. When you are grieved over missed opportunities, wasted resources and foolish pursuits, you become open to a better way. You know that God has something greater in store and you long for His best. Godly sorrow helps us decide that trusting Jesus is better.

If you feel guilty, take that emotion captive. Press into it and ask God to reveal where the guilt is coming from. Do not react out of guilt. Choose a better way. Ask God to show you His will, then allow yourself to experience godly sorrow in regards to any ungodly attitudes you have.

Godly sorrow leads to repentance, and repentance leads to change. Is God working on your heart for a lifestyle change?

5. "I'm a tither. I've got this giving thing down. If all these slackers would just get on board, we would never have to talk about money again."

Of all of the things said regarding talking about money in church, this one is probably the worst. The arrogance and pride that is associated with this line of thinking is more destructive than all of the others combined.

> "Pride goes before destruction, a haughty spirit before a fall."
>
> **Proverbs 16:18**

True giving leaders are humble and gracious. They understand the struggle that most face in regard to giving. They are not judgmental, mean-spirited, or holier-than-thou. Irritation with those who do not give is a sure sign that something is wrong in your heart.

The struggle with giving is exponentially increased when there are people looking down on others. This type of behavior only produces guilt. God's kindness is what leads us to repentance. Faithful givers must be humble enough to allow God's kindness to be expressed through them.

Christ followers are to be life-long learners who never stop growing. Sadly, many people stop growing in regard to giving because they believe that they have reached some kind of pinnacle of generosity. When was the last time you prayerfully reevaluated your giving?

Are you growing as a giver? Are you willing to ask God to show you what percentage of your income is generous, or have you already made up your mind what the number is? Check yourself before you wreck your church.

The best thing to do when your mind starts to spin out of control is to pray. Stop and ask God to give you clarity in your thinking. Ask God to guide your thoughts. Ask God to speak to you.

Right now, will you pray a bold prayer?

"God, show me what percentage of my income is generous. Amen."

chapter two

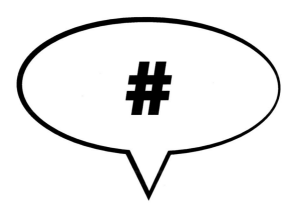

W<small>HAT</small> is your magic number?

How much money do you need to make your problems go away? How much money do you need to fix your marriage, ease your stress, resolve your health issues, save your business, fix your family, or retire your debt?

Almost everyone holds some version of the magic number deep within. We think, "If I just had $_____$, things would be so much better." "If I won the lottery, I would _____ and finally be happy." "I'm not greedy...I just need $_____ to get by so that money would no longer be an issue."

So what's your magic number? How much would it take to bring peace to your life? How much would it take to let you sleep soundly at night? How much would it take to really set you free?

Maybe it is the amount that would get you out of credit card debt or would pay off your mortgage or would send your kids to college or would finance your retirement dreams. For some, it is $1,000; for others, it is $10,000 or $100,000 or $1 million. The funny thing about the magic number is that it never goes away. What would happen if you got the amount of money you believe you need? How long would it take before a new magic number came into the picture?

It is tempting to think that money will solve our problems. If we could just accumulate enough wealth, everything would be okay— there would be no more trials. It is easy to believe that more money could save our marriages, make our children happier, and bring us the lasting soul satisfaction that we all so desperately crave, but it just isn't true.

We buy the lie that says money makes everything better. When we pursue money, money begins to dominate us. It dominates our time, energy, dreams and devotion. Our emotions are tied to money. We base our decisions primarily on money. We place our hope in money. For all intents and purposes, money becomes our god.

This is an idolatry issue. Money is the #1 false god in our world and by now you ought to know that money makes a terrible god. Just take a look at a dollar bill. Right across the top is says, "In God we trust." There is a reminder on our money, but still we forget.

Money is fleeting. Jobs are lost. Fortunes are squandered. Stock markets crash. Economic systems collapse. Kingdoms crumble. And even if you could hold onto wealth until death, what would happen then? You can't take it with you. In the end (and the end is coming), only one God will remain…and His name is not money.

The issue of idolatry is a big deal to God. That is why He mentions it first in the Ten Commandments.

"You shall have no other gods before me."
Exodus 20:3

God understands how idolatry divides the human heart, and He reminds us that this is always the ultimate issue. Think about what Jesus said when He was asked about the greatest commandment.

"Jesus replied: 'Love the Lord your God with all your heart and with all your soul and with all your mind.' This is the first and greatest commandment."
Matthew 22:37-38

Jesus also spoke directly about the issue of money competing with God for supremacy in our hearts.

"No one can serve two masters. Either you will hate the one and love the other, or you will be devoted to the one and despise the other. You cannot serve both God and money."
Matthew 6:24

You can't do it. You cannot serve both God and money. We deceive ourselves and believe that we can balance God and money in our hearts, but we can't. In the end we wind up using God to serve money. Our prayers are not humble submissions of self to do God's will. They become hollow requests for more. We replace "Here I am, use me" with "Where are you? Give me..."

We treat Almighty God like a cosmic vending machine in the sky. When He doesn't dispense what we feel we deserve, we shake, pound, kick and walk away disgusted.

And even when we give, it is often out of some perverted give-to-get notion. We think, "I'll give to God so He will give to me." We treat God like a wealth management strategy that savvy investors know how to manipulate in just the right way.

All of the terrible things Christians have done with money…from the selling of indulgences to the health-and-wealth prosperity preaching… have been attempts to use God to serve money. It happens at the global level, the local level and the individual level. No one is immune. We cannot serve God and money.

But we can use money to serve God.

Giving generously to God puts money in its place. Money is a real world reality. We cannot ignore it. We must intentionally use money or money will use us.

Pay attention. Look for signs that idolatry is creeping into your heart. Money becomes a God-substitute when we expect it to provide things we should receive from our relationship with God.

Consider these five things we often expect money to give us instead of trusting God to provide.

1. Motivation

Money is an idol when it becomes your primary source of motivation.

Why do you get up in the morning? Do you rise and shine to give God glory and to serve Him throughout the day, or do you grudgingly roll out bed each day thinking, "Another day, another dollar"?

Why do you go to work or school? Are you driven by the almighty dollar or the Almighty God? Think about how we ingrain this type of motivation into our children. We tell them, "You have to go to school, so you can make good grades, so you can get into a good college, so you can get a good job, so you can make a good living." We make money a motivation for our children, but do we present glorifying God as a more important motivator for them?

How do you make decisions? Do you seek God first and ask what He desires before you consider the financial ramifications? How did you decide where to work or where to live? Think about a recent purchase. What factors did you consider before making the purchase? At what point, if any, did you ask God what He wanted you to do?

It is tempting to get defensive and to make excuses about living in the real world. Do you really understand what the real world is? If you believe that money makes the world go 'round, then I contend that you cannot see the real world. God makes the world go 'round. Money is merely a created thing that only possesses whatever power we allow it to have.

Money must be put in its proper place. Make pleasing God your primary motivator and use money to glorify Him.

2. Comfort

Much is revealed when we turn to money for comfort instead of God. Essentially we are telling God that His comfort is insufficient. We reject what He offers in order to pursue comfort in material possessions; we choose false gods over the real God.

It is impossible to follow Jesus when our primary concern is lifestyle development and maintenance. When we choose comfortable lifestyles and easy living over Jesus, we reveal what (not whom) we truly worship.

Remember what Jesus said about being His disciple.

"Then Jesus said to his disciples, 'Whoever wants to be my disciple must deny themselves and take up their cross and follow me. For whoever wants to save their life will lose it, but whoever loses their life for me will find it. What good will it be for someone to gain the

whole world, yet forfeit their soul? Or what can anyone give in exchange for their soul?'"
Matthew 16:24-26

There is always some discomfort in cross-carrying adventures. When following Jesus gets difficult (and it always gets difficult), it is tempting to lay down our crosses in order to grab hold of some phony version of comfort. Jesus warns us that this is pointless. What good would it do for you to build the most comfortable, easy-living lifestyle in the history of the world and yet forfeit your very soul?

God's comfort is eternal. It does not diminish over time. It does not break. It never disappoints.

3. Security

Fear is a very real thing. I do not buy into the "False Evidence Appearing Real" acronym for fear. People use that acronym in attempts to ease fear, but the truth of the matter is that this world is a pretty scary place. There are many real fear-producing things that we encounter every day.

Fear is magnified when we look for security in something that is incapable of providing it. If your security revolves around money, then you are in for one topsy-turvy ride.

How secure do you feel in your job? People lose jobs all the time. Companies fold. Mistakes are made. Coworkers stab each other in the back. Economic shifts bring changes that nobody could see coming and entire industries vanish. Your job does not offer real security.

How secure do you feel in your home? People lose their homes every day. Natural disasters and fires reduce homes to rubble overnight. People become ill and cannot work. They fall behind on their mortgages and the banks are forced to foreclose. Marriages fall apart, and once-happy homes become bargaining chips in divorce proceedings. So we lock our doors and arm our alarm systems to create the illusion of security, but deep down the fear does not fade.

How secure do you feel with your bank account? How many months' income do you have in reserve? How is that retirement plan looking? How about the kids' college fund? Good planning and saving are important, but do they actually secure your future?

God reminds us over and over again in the scriptures to "fear not." He wants to give us security, but until we turn to Him, fear will rule the day.

4. Joy

All of us think we want to be happy, but what we really want is sustaining joy. Happiness is circumstantial and fades quickly. Joy, on the other hand, is derived from inner-peace that radiates outward and does not diminish when difficulties arise.

The fleeting nature of money cannot produce the joy we desire. When we turn to money in hopes that it will provide joy, we are always disappointed. What happens when the vacation ends and you have to go back to the daily grind? What happens when the new car smell wears off and is replaced with some mystery funk you cannot seem to locate? What happens when the newest version of technology makes your latest purchase virtually obsolete?

You know what happens. Sadness ensues.

Things…money, possessions and purchases cannot provide joy. It is foolish to think otherwise. God is the joy-provider. He is the one who brings peace to the core of our being. He longs to give us His joy, but we must intentionally receive it, remember it and revive it. This is why we are commanded to rejoice in the Lord.

> *"Rejoice in the Lord always. I will say it again: Rejoice!"*
>
> **Philippians 4:4**

God tells us to actively rejoice in Him so that we do not misplace our efforts to find joy by looking elsewhere. Rejoice in the Lord always. Return to Him for joy in all things at all times. Remember who you are in Him and what He has done for you. Allow His joy to sustain you so you are not tempted to turn to a god-substitute.

5. Identity

Who are you?

Think about our social interactions and how we describe who we are to others. After saying our names we typically talk about what we do for a living, where we live, where our kids go to school, and then look for common ground with whomever we are speaking.

When you think about who you are, does your relationship with Jesus come to mind? If you were asked to describe yourself, would there be any reference to being a follower of Jesus? If you are a Christian, then you have a new identity.

"So from now on we regard no one from a worldly point of view. Though we once regarded Christ in this way, we do so no longer. Therefore, if anyone is in Christ, the new creation has come: The old has gone, the new is here!"

2 Corinthians 5:16-17

We must no longer look at identity from a worldly point of view. The worldly view of identity is firmly rooted in money.

Consider identity theft. What does someone get if they take your identity? They steal your money and your purchasing power. Culturally we are convinced that identity is primarily about what we can own.

It is also interesting to think about how we see people as being good or bad based on their financial position. Deep down we know this to be untrue and we quickly deny any prejudice against people whose socio-economic status is lower than our own. But just follow this common line of thinking: "Rich people are good. Poor people are bad. Rich people have good jobs, live in good neighborhoods, drive good cars, and send their kids to good schools. Poor people have bad jobs, live in bad neighborhoods, drive bad cars, and send their kids to bad schools."

We unknowingly transfer our feelings about money to people because we view identity in terms of economic possibilities. I think about this often and would love to claim that I am immune to the foolishness of this worldview, but truth be told, I am not. I had the following experience while writing this book.

My family went to the Basketball Hall of Fame in Springfield, Massachusetts. After enjoying the exhibits and a long day of fun, we walked out into the parking lot. It was a slow day at the Basketball Hall of Fame and there were not many cars in the lot, but off in the distance I noticed an old, beat-up car driving toward us. I immediately pulled my youngest daughter in tight and said to the family, "Look out, here comes a crazy driver."

As the car slowed down and went safely by us, I looked at the driver and realized what I had done. I had decided that the driver was a bad driver based solely on the age and condition of her car. The car was not going too fast or out of control. There was nothing to indicate that the driver was unsafe, but my mind associated good driving with good cars and bad driving with bad cars.

If we do not view identity first and foremost in regard to who we are in Christ, we will make all kinds of awful judgments. We even begin to think about God's blessings in terms of financial success. If someone is rich, we say that God blessed that person. Money is not a blessing or a curse. How we handle money is what makes the blessing or curse.

Who you are determines what you will do. Do you understand that you are an adopted child of the Most High God…that you share in His eternal kingdom…that you are called to be a part of His business to seek and save the lost? You are not a number in a bank account, an address on a street, or a credit score. If you belong to Jesus, then you have an identity that can never be taken, lost, or thrown away.

> *"Do not store up for yourselves treasures on earth, where moths and vermin destroy, and where thieves break in and steal. But store up for yourselves treasures in heaven, where moths and vermin do not destroy, and where thieves do not break in and steal. For where your treasure is, there your heart will be also."*
> **Matthew 6:19-21**

You cannot serve both God and money, but you can use money to serve God. Is God #1 or is money #1? That is really the only number that matters.

chapter three

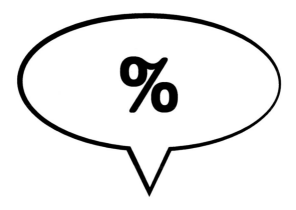

WARNING: What you are about to read is not for the faint of heart. If you wish to remain in the throes of socially-acceptable idolatry, then please quietly close this book and quickly walk away. To continue reading means that ignorance will be driven from your repertoire of excuses. You will know the truth, and the truth will set you free.

Being set free does not mean you will be free. Freedom is still a choice. God can throw the prison doors open, but you still have to walk out. Knowing the truth reveals the path to freedom, but it takes courage to leave the prison behind. I know from personal experience how it feels to be set free, but choose to remain in bondage. I knew the principles of percentage-based giving for years before I conjured up enough courage to actually leave the god of my youth, my friends, and my ancestors behind. I pray that this will not be the case for you.

Freedom from money worship is available. The solution is simple, but it is not easy. What I am going to share with you will likely offend you, irritate you, anger you, and produce scoffing of epic proportions.

Why?

Why do we feel offended when challenged to give money? Why do we get defensive and disengage from reasonable thought? Why do we scoff and ignore biblical precedent, 2,000 years of church history, and personal testimonies from genuine people?

We respond this way when what we worship is attacked, and I assure you that what you are about to read (assuming that you are still reading) is a full-fledged assault on the god of money. You must decide whether or not to allow this to happen. Are you willing to engage in thought that could radically alter your entire world-view and change the trajectory of your life?

Yes – this is a big deal. No – I am not overstating the importance of what I am about to share.

Percentage-based giving is God's answer to the idolatry of money worship.

Please understand that this is God's answer, not my answer. I did not make this up. Percentage-based giving is not my invention. In fact, some have warned me not to share this. They say that it won't work, that it is too upsetting, that it is too counter-cultural.

I must share it though. If I did not have to, I wouldn't. If it were really up to me, I'd probably just give you a spoonful of sugar and skip the medicine all together. We could all waste away together in the Candyland of excess we falsely call reality.

Oh, but I know this truth, and this truth is mixed with God's love moving through me. Together they form an explosive mixture that

I cannot contain. The words of the prophet Jeremiah come to mind.

> *"But if I say, 'I will not mention his word or speak anymore in his name,' his word is in my heart like a fire, a fire shut up in my bones.*
> *I am weary of holding it in; indeed, I cannot.*
> *I hear many whispering, 'Terror on every side! Denounce him! Let's denounce him!' All my friends are waiting for me to slip, saying, 'Perhaps he will be deceived; then we will prevail over him and take our revenge on him.'"*
>
> **Jeremiah 20:9-10**

I know what people want me to say. Some want to hear that percentage-based giving is not a New Testament principle. They want to believe that God maintains some separation of church and bank account. Others will argue that percentage-based giving is not hard line enough. They want to bring back the Old Testament temple tax and prosecute the lawbreakers who do not tithe.

I am an equal opportunity offender. The hardcore tithers will hate this because it will not feed into their legalistic, prideful notions of comparative holiness. The anti-tithers will hate this because it will not let them off the hook from obeying God's clear desire for His people to participate in percentage-based giving. I am not going to make anyone happy, but if delusional happiness was my primary agenda, then I would write a book about puppies, rainbows and lollipops.

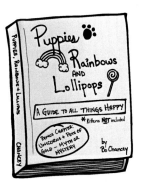

Percentage-based giving is biblical, practical, and worshipful. Tithe simply means ten percent. Tithing is percentage-based giving. The first example of percentage-based giving is found in Genesis when Abraham gave a tenth to the priest Melchizedek.

"Then Melchizedek king of Salem brought out bread and wine. He was priest of God Most High, and he blessed Abram, saying, 'Blessed be Abram by God Most High, Creator of heaven and earth. And praise be to God Most High, who delivered your enemies into your hand.' Then Abram gave him a tenth of everything."

Genesis 14:18-20

Generosity expressed through percentage-based giving existed before Moses, the Exodus, and the Law. It was a responsive act of worship, trust, and devotion. Abraham received from God, so He gave back to God. He was not commanded by God to do so, and he was under no obligation. Abraham is the father of our faith and his example of percentage-based giving is well worth emulating.

From Genesis to Malachi, giving ten percent of income to God is commanded and practiced over and over again. Abraham did it, the Law commanded it, the kings supported it, and the prophets backed it up. Consider how strongly percentage-based giving is communicated in the last book of the Old Testament.

"'I the LORD do not change. So you, the descendants of Jacob, are not destroyed.

Ever since the time of your ancestors you have turned away from my decrees and have not kept them. Return to me, and I will return to you,' says the LORD Almighty.
'But you ask, "How are we to return?"
'Will a mere mortal rob God? Yet you rob me.
'But you ask, "How are we robbing you?"
'In tithes and offerings. You are under a curse— your whole nation—because you are robbing me. Bring the whole tithe into the storehouse, that there may be food in my house. Test me in this,' says the LORD Almighty, 'and see if I will not throw open the floodgates of heaven and pour out so much blessing that there will not be room enough to store it.'"

Malachi 3:6-10

God does not change. He is slow to anger and rich in love. He is patient with us, but loves us enough to communicate difficult truth. God wants people to return to Him. He knows the allure that the god of money has on the human heart. God longs for us to cling to Him, but this cannot happen until we let go of money. Giving freely to God demonstrates our love for Him.

It comes down to trust. Do we trust the provision or the provider? God is able to provide in ways that we cannot even begin to imagine.

I went to a movie with my three children and they wanted some snacks from the concession stand. I was feeling generous, so I splurged on the wickedly over-priced candy, popcorn and sodas. I was not particularly hungry, so I did not purchase anything for myself.

When we were seated and the lights went out, I realized I had made a mistake. I wanted a little taste of the bountiful snacks I had provided for my children, so I leaned over and asked each of them to share. Now, how do you think they responded?

They all said the same four-letter word, "M-I-N-E!"

Mine? Are you kidding me? They said, "Mine!" We needed to have a little chat.

I explained right then and there that the only reason they had snacks was that their benevolent father wanted to bless them. They held nothing in their greedy little hands that I had not provided, and I had power to provide much, much more. I pulled out my credit card and said, "Do you see this? I can go to that concession stand anytime I want and buy every snack they have in there. I could bury you in a mountain of popcorn and candy if I wanted to. I could give you more of that stuff than you could ever possibly consume. I am capable of buying my own, and I am big enough and strong enough to take yours anytime I want, but I would rather you share with me."

When I asked if they understood, all three nodded in wide-eyed comprehension. Every few minutes throughout the movie one of them would willingly offer me some candy or popcorn. They got it because it made sense.

Do you get it? Does it make sense?

God is the provider. He provides and entrusts His provisions to us. He gives us free will to decide what we will do with it, but He knows how our hearts wander. We are tempted to trust the provision over the provider. Percentage-based giving is His answer. God even says to test Him on this. He says, "Try me and see what I can do. You have a choice. You can go your own way and try to manage on your own, or you can trust me and enjoy all that I provide."

Percentage-based giving is also a New Testament concept. It is true that we are no longer held to fulfilling the Old Testament Law. Jesus completed that through His work on the cross and His resurrection. We are not bound by a legalistic, Old Testament tithe, but New Testament teaching drives the principle of percentage-based giving home.

Jesus never says not to tithe. When He did mention it, His comment was that they should continue.

> "Woe to you, teachers of the law and Pharisees, you hypocrites! You give a tenth of your spices—mint, dill and cumin. But you have neglected the more important matters of the law—justice, mercy and faithfulness. You should have practiced the latter, without neglecting the former."
> **Matthew 23:23**

The only downside to tithing is when it is used as a replacement for the righteousness that God desires. Tithing can be a self-righteous activity and Jesus strictly forbids all forms of self-righteousness. Percentage-based giving is better than legalistic tithing because it demands we ask God what He wants us to do instead of assuming we already know. Percentage-based giving is based on our relationship with God. We must seek Him and listen to His answer about what to give.

This scares the bajeebers out of people because of the possibility of human error. We can mishear God, lie about His answer, or deceive ourselves into thinking that He does not answer. Yes, these are very real possibilities, but we are always encouraged to seek clarity from God in prayer.

Pray a bold prayer: "God, show me what percentage of my income is generous."

Listen and obey. When in doubt fall back on the biblical norm of ten percent until you hear differently. The important thing is to seek God's will in this matter.

> *"Each of you should give what you have decided in your heart to give, not reluctantly or under compulsion, for God loves a cheerful giver. And God is able to bless you abundantly, so that in all things at all times, having all that you need, you will abound in every good work."*
> **2 Corinthians 9:7-8**

Each of us should give. Giving is for everyone. Nobody is exempt from the blessing and joy of giving to the Lord. Giving is for the rich, the poor and everyone in between.

Give what you have decided in your heart to give. Make a decision. Have a plan. Ask God what He wants you to give and then do it.

Do not give reluctantly or under compulsion. Percentage-based giving provides great freedom. You make a decision about what percentage is generous, and then you give it right off the top. No questions asked. You give out of God's abundant provision instead of your meager leftovers. When giving is the first thing you do with money, it becomes the most joyful thing you do with money.

God loves a cheerful giver. Do you feel God's pleasure in the way you handle the money He entrusts to you? It is not that God will love you less if you refuse to give, but when we refuse to give, it places a rift in our relationship with God. Giving tightens the bond and draws us close to Him because it demonstrates trust and worship.

God is able. You do not need to be afraid. He can provide whatever you need. Is it more foolish to trust God and give, or to trust self and withhold?

When you give, you will abound in every good work. God's provision is not for selfish gain but so we can abound in the work He calls us to.

"Now about the collection for the Lord's people: Do what I told the Galatian churches to do. On the first day of every week, each one of you should set aside a sum of money in keeping with your income, saving it up, so that when I come no collections will have to be made."

1 Corinthians 16:1-2

Paul tells the church in Corinth to give a percentage of their income each week so that no special collections would need to be made. Percentage-based giving is better than reactionary giving. Reactionary giving is almost never as generous as planned, percentage-based giving. One-time, responsive gifts typically do not add up to much of a percentage. We like to believe we are generous when we give to causes and respond to needs, but a plan is needed in order to actually give a generous percentage of income.

Realistically add up all of the contributions you make to various needs throughout the year. How much is it really? What is the total number? What percent of your income are you giving away?

Ask God to show you what percentage of your income is generous. Listen for His response. Obey.

Refrain from the folly of formulating phony excuses.

For a long time, I thought that I could not afford to give a percentage of my income to God. I held onto the belief that I was underpaid and my budget was already maxed. I lived under a curse and did not enjoy the blessing of percentage-based giving.

It all started with my first job out of college. My wife and I were newlyweds and I went to work for an amazing church. We made the decision to accept a much lower salary than we were offered from other churches because we believed God was calling us to be a part of what He was doing at that particular church.

The leaders of the church were aware that our income was low, and a couple of them spoke to me regarding their concern. In an attempt to be kind, they told me that we did not need to give because my income was so small. When they said it to me, I knew that what they were saying was wrong. I knew that it contradicted scripture, the heart of Jesus, and what the Holy Spirit was revealing to me. I knew all of that, but chose to believe their sentiment anyway.

My family lived under that curse for years. When I refer to a curse, I do not mean that an angry, vengeful God was raining down lightning bolts of fury on us because of our disobedience. I am simply referring to the natural consequences of sin.

I missed out on the blessings of giving. I did not rejoice when the church rejoiced over the generosity that God displayed through their giving. I felt guilty and defensive every time giving came up in conversations or sermons. I was angry, bitter, and resentful about my compensation. I blamed others. The church was to blame because they did not pay me enough.

My wife was to blame because she spent too much. My friends were to blame because they put pressure on me to live a lifestyle I could not afford. My parents were to blame because they did not give us a chunk of money to start us off financially on the right foot.

I was under a curse and the curse impacted every relationship.

I remember being asked once what I would do if the church I worked for was forced to reduce staff and they had to let some go, but I could stay with an eight percent cut in pay. What would I do? Was there a way I could make that work? This hypothetical scenario really got me thinking. It was the first step to breaking the curse because I became aware that if we had to, we could live with less. Sure, we would need to make some lifestyle adjustments, but it would not be the end of the world.

I began to give. It was sporadic at first, and fear still filled my heart. When things looked tight, I withheld my giving. Those years were filled with financial fear. We never felt like we would have enough, but my disobedience in giving made praying boldly virtually impossible.

My trust in God waned each time I chose money over Him.

But things changed. We finally had enough of the curse and longed for God's blessing of freedom. We asked God to show us what percentage of our income was generous. We heard from Him, and we obeyed. We set up our giving online so that our offering is the first thing that goes out of our bank account each time we get paid. We periodically ask God to show us if the percentage He wants us to give has changed, and we go in and up our giving. We are having a blast!

I heard rumors over the years that giving was fun, but there was no way for me to understand until I actually did it. Each year the percentage we give to the church grows, but we also find that we give more now than ever to other causes. I did not see that coming, but when money is put in its proper place, all of a sudden you are free to use it to generously serve God in all kinds of ways.

I share my story with you because stories are important. They testify to who God is and how He works. Over the years, I heard story after story about how percentage-based giving radically changed lives. Genuine people spoke to me about the freedom this discipline unleashed for them. They were willing to be used by God to testify to His goodness even if it meant stepping on toes and saying unpopular things. I am thankful to God that He used them in my life.

One reaction I sometimes get when sharing about our giving journey is people kind of assume giving is easy for me because I am a pastor. I have actually had people say to me, "Well, you are a pastor, so of course you give. That stuff doesn't work in the real world." First of all, I live in the real world. It is not like they wrap me up, place me in storage, and wheel me out on Sunday mornings to preach. I deal with financial pressures. I deal with a mortgage, college funds, retirement planning, and the day-to-day consumption that dominates our culture. Secondly, you try giving 8%, 10%, 12%, 15% of your paycheck back to your employer with no strings attached. Percentage-based giving is hard at first. I understand.

Generously give money to God with no strings attached. This is not a give-to-get sales pitch. The reward that God offers is not an exponential increase in your bank account, recognition for being an awesome benefactor, or a legacy of things attached to your name (there are no memorial scholarships, buildings bearing your name, or "donated by" plaques in your future). The reward is freedom from idolatry.

Is that enough? If not, it seems reasonable to ask the most pressing question at hand. Is Jesus truly Lord of your life?

If you hold to the claim that money is not a false god for you, then prove it. Don't prove it to me. You owe me nothing. Don't prove it to God. He already knows where your heart is. Prove it to yourself. Demonstrate your freedom from the #1, all-time, greatest idol in the history of the world.

How?

Give a generous percentage of your income to God. Do it consistently and watch what happens.

Pray, "God show me what percentage of my income is generous. Amen."

chapter four

Most people love a good deal. We are programmed to negotiate and manipulate so that we are on the winning side of transactions. It is often said that if you do not know who is on the losing side of a business deal, then it is definitely you.

We share our money-saving exploits with great pride and conviction. "I saved $20 on these shoes. I saved $400 on this television. I saved $5,000 on this car. I won. I am the winner. Look at how much I saved!"

But how much did you have to spend in order to save?

We buy into a system that convinces us we are saving when in reality we are spending. We are programmed to consume things we do not need and probably do not even want. Over-consumption leads to issues like addiction, gluttony and selfishness.

This is not a good deal. We are not winning. We consume and accumulate, but for what?

There is a bumper sticker with the quote, "Whoever dies with the most toys, wins." At first glance, the quote seems funny, cute and clever, but in reality it represents a deadly mindset. Entire lives are spent accumulating toys.

Why? Well…whoever has the most stuff… wins. And, don't we all want to win?

But what is the prize? It is just a toy chest filled with broken down toys nobody wants to play with anymore.

Today's treasure is tomorrow's trash. Everything we purchase winds up in the dump.

It breaks down, wears out, goes out of fashion, or we simply lose interest and move on to the next toy. Consuming never leads to any type of lasting soul satisfaction. It merely provides a temporary buzz…an addict's fix that quickly wears off until you can find your next score.

Jesus warns us about how crazy it is to live like this.

> "Do not store up for yourselves treasures on earth, where moths and vermin destroy, and where thieves break in and steal. But store up for yourselves treasures in heaven, where moths and vermin do not destroy, and where thieves do not break in and steal. For where your treasure is, there your heart will be also."
>
> **Matthew 6:19-21**

Jesus does not want your heart to go to the dump! He says, "Where your treasure is, your heart will be also." All of that treasure is heading to the same destination and our hearts are bound to follow. Identities that are based on what we own, will ultimately become worthless. That kind of identity holds no value for eternity and winds up in the trash.

Jesus wants our hearts to be with Him. But how do we do that? Jesus said that our hearts follow our treasure. A simple look at a bank statement reveals our priorities. Follow the money to see what is important. Necessities like lodging, transportation, food and clothing are typically near the top. Entertainment, savings for retirement, and things required for lifestyle maintenance are easy to identify and quantify. We can see what percentage of our income goes to each of these things and have a pretty good idea of what we value most.

Where does giving to God come into the equation? If we do not know the answer to that question, we are far more likely to drift on the sea of consumerism. Percentage-based giving sets our hearts on God and provides a fixed point of reference for all other uses of money.

Planned, percentage-based giving points our hearts in the right direction. It is a matter of first things first.

"So do not worry, saying, 'What shall we eat?' or 'What shall we drink?' or 'What shall we wear?' For the pagans run after all these things, and your heavenly Father knows that you need them.

But seek first his kingdom and his righteousness, and all these things will be given to you as well."
Matthew 6:31-33

Money worries are awful. Fear regarding the scarcity of resources drives us to do foolish things. Relationships are ruined over money worries. Families are destroyed. Friendships end. But the most tragic of all is when money worries drive you away from God. Jesus said that you cannot serve two masters. You cannot serve God and money. You will love one and hate the other. One or the other must be first. Which is first in your life? God or money? How do you know?

Planned, percentage-based giving puts money in its proper place. When God is truly number one in your life you can be free from money worries. He knows what you need and is completely capable of providing. Seek Him first by actively giving and you can walk out of the prison of worry.

This does not mean that you will get whatever you want. There is clearly a difference between wants and needs. God provides our needs, but He also transforms our wants. Giving changes your priorities and your wants follow. Giving is so counter-cultural that it is difficult to overstate the power that it unleashes. In a consumer-driven world, giving is a mind-blower. But when you make the transition from consumer to giver, your entire worldview changes. This is why Jesus said to seek first His Kingdom and His righteousness.

Planned, percentage-based giving puts God first. When the first thing you do with any bit of income is give a portion of it to God, you are on your way to amazing freedom and fruitful living. Seek Jesus first and allow Him to take care of you.

Why is that a scary thought for so many? Consider how many people claim to trust Jesus with the eternal salvation of their souls, but refuse to trust Him with money. It is ludicrous to trust Jesus with the ultimate thing and then not trust Him in the minor things. That is stinking thinking.

Seek Jesus first AND...

And what?

AND...all these things will be given to you as well.

That seems like a good deal, but truthfully most are repulsed by it. Why? Well, the reason why is that we do not want it given to us. We want to earn it. When we earn it, we feel like winners. It is a control issue. Will I trust God or myself?

You may be one of the most amazing people who has ever lived, but you are not even close to being as amazing as God. When we trust self over God, we have every reason to worry.

"Then Jesus said to his disciples: "Therefore I tell you, do not worry about your life, what you will eat; or about your body, what you will wear. For life is more than food, and the body more than clothes. Consider the ravens: They do not sow or reap, they have no storeroom or barn; yet God feeds them. And how much more valuable you are than birds! Who of you by worrying can add a single hour to your life? Since you cannot do this very little thing, why do you worry about the rest?"

Luke 12:22-26

I can tell you right now how this whole thing is going to end. You are going to die. You cannot stop it. Death is coming. You have zero control over that outcome. Worrying will not change it.

Scripture is clear about the wages of sin being death. All have sinned and all will die. But the gift of God is eternal life through Christ Jesus our Lord. Physical death is a beginning not an end. Jesus offers an amazing deal. We give Him our sin and He gives us eternal life. We trade our death for life. This is the greatest deal in the history of the world.

We do not deserve the gift of salvation. We cannot earn it. We do not control it. God gives it. He gives His Son to save us. We win, but only through Jesus. We do not win on our own merit or effort.

Seek first His kingdom and His righteousness AND...

And you will value what God values.

And you will want what God wants.

And you will do what God does.

You will give and give and give and life will explode with passion and purpose.

This is the true reward for giving to God. Too many people assume that when you give to God that He will magically remove every financial struggle and make you filthy rich. Giving is not some kind of give to get pyramid scheme. Yes, God blesses people who faithfully give, but those blessings are not necessarily monetary in nature. In fact, who says more money is even a blessing? Some know it to be a curse.

I hear Christians refer to wealthy people as being blessed by God. That is not necessarily the case. Managing wealth for God's glory can be a major burden.

The real blessings of God are eternal in nature and have more to do with building His kingdom than any kind of monetary gain.

Give to God AND you will trust Him like you never have before. Giving is one of the greatest faith builders. When you give, you release your trust in money and put it in God. It is a way of going all in. Giving is a way to demonstrate your faith in God's provision over your abilities.

Give to God AND He gives you peace. Money worries dissipate with giving. Money problems will probably still occur, but you will be freed from worrying. The trust you have in God produces tremendous peace. You know that He is good and that He will provide for your needs. Your identity in Him is secure and you are not afraid.

Give to God AND you will worship with undeniable freedom. Your heart will not be divided. You can worship without holding back or struggling with guilt. Anger and fear will fall off you and you will exalt God with great passion.

Give to God AND your prayers will get bolder. You will not hold back, but will make bold requests of God that are more often in line with His will. The barrier of greed will be removed and you will not be ashamed to present your requests to God.

Give to God AND you will know that your identity is rooted in Him. Knowing who you are is crucial for deciding what you will do. When you put God first in regards to money, He is far more likely to be first in every other aspect of your life.

God is a loving Father who knows what is best for His children. He is able to take care of you and He knows how to best bless us. His love is perfect even when ours fails.

> *"Which of you, if your son asks for bread, will give him a stone? Or if he asks for a fish, will give him a snake? If you, then, though you are evil, know how to give good gifts to your children, how much more will your Father in heaven give good gifts to those who ask him!"*
> **Matthew 7:9-11**

God's gifts are good. They are better than we could ever imagine. He knows exactly how to give us what we need...not too much and not too little. Our God's love is perfect and is expressed perfectly, because He knows us perfectly.

I love my children, but my love is far from perfect. There is still way too much of me being expressed in my love for them. I project myself and my baggage onto my kids. It is not intentional, but I am aware enough to know that I must watch out for it.

When my son, Ace, started getting an allowance for doing chores he was excited about all of the possible things he could do with his money. He talked about the things he would buy and the places he would go. After dreaming out loud for a bit he stopped and said, "The first thing I'm going to do is give 25% to the church."

What kind of response do you think that statement evoked in me? Do you think I felt pride or satisfaction? Do you think I immediately responded in an encouraging way by telling him that sounded like a great idea? Well…I didn't.

My first response was to think, "That's too much!" Thankfully I did not say that out loud, but it is what I thought. I almost threw down a curse on my son, because of my own fears about money. This was the first time we had ever spoken about him giving to the church and I almost totally blew it. He came up with that number. Nobody had said it to him or suggested it. It was the number he felt was generous and right and I almost ruined it.

God got a hold of my heart before I could wreck the moment and I simply replied, "That sounds great buddy. You should give generously to God and enjoy it." We then sat down to figure out how much money 25% would be each week and came up with a plan for how he would give it.

Ask God what percentage of your income is generous. Listen to His response and then give that percentage joyfully. Your heavenly Father will receive your offering and your relationship with Him will grow. You will be open to receive His good and perfect gifts. You will feel His pleasure and experience an increase in the things that matter most...things like love, joy, peace, patience, kindness, goodness, faithfulness, gentleness and self-control.

chapter five

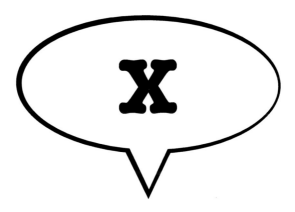

Our culture grooms us to be consummate consumers. We are trained, programmed and resourced to consume. Our economic system depends on a consumer-driven populace. The continual desire for more, bigger, better and newer keeps our world going 'round.

But is there a limit to how much we can consume? Is there a point where the system collapses?

My son wanted me to take him back-to-school shopping. My kids are convinced that back-to-school shopping is a necessary rite of passage for each new school year. In the same way, they think Black Friday is an actual holiday. They have seriously asked me, "Dad, how are we going to celebrate Black Friday this year?"

Anyway, the boy said to me, "Dad, I know where you need to take me back-to-school shopping this year." He then proceeded to tell me the name of a sporting goods store he saw in a commercial. They had all his favorite brands and were having a great sale. He explained that we should go quickly before they ran out of the good stuff.

Without thinking, I just kind of nodded my head in agreement like it was some forgone conclusion that back-to-school shopping would occur. Then reality set in. My son needs NOTHING in the way of clothes. The dude has more clothes than he could ever wear. His room is a solid three-feet deep in clothes with every drawer filled and the closet stuffed. We have bags of clothes in our garage that we have not even gone through yet. He has enough clothing options that he could wear a different outfit each day of the year.

How did this happen?

Well…it just kind of snuck up on us. We have a couple of friends who have boys who have grown rapidly. Their rapid growth has meant a steady supply of hand-me-downs to our son. We receive a generous bounty of barely, if ever, worn clothes from two sources. In addition, we continue to purchase him clothes without considering what we already have.

I feel like a fool, and honestly, I should. I acted foolishly. I did what I was programmed to do. I consumed. I consumed to my own detriment. Over-consumption hurts, but we easily ignore what is obvious and go down paths that lead to greed, gluttony and lust.

It is interesting to consider how our consumption has grown. My dad was born in the 1940s and when he was a kid, he got one pair of shoes each year. I was born in the 1970s, and I got three pairs of shoes for each year… one pair of dress shoes, one pair of school shoes, and one pair of older shoes for playing outside. My son was born in the 2000s, and he currently has 15 pairs of shoes. He has shoes for every activity…church shoes, casual shoes, boat shoes, basketball shoes, golf shoes, running shoes, slip-ons, lace-ups and boots. We have shoes coming out the wazoo, but I do not think we have ever once considered the absurdity of it. After all, his friends all have that many pairs of shoes, and the T.V. said we should buy more.

Our culture programs us to consume, but God calls us to invest. Giving is radically counter-cultural because it directly impacts our ability to consume. A battle is raging for your identity. Will you allow God to determine your identity, or will you conform to the cultural norm? Do you want your primary identity in God's economy to be that of a consumer or an investor?

Consumers consume. Investors invest.

Consumers suck resources and produce waste. Investors give resources and produce growth.

The typical mindset of most Christians is that it is God's job to give and our job to consume. God gives grace and we consume it. God gives love and we consume it. God gives life and we consume it. We consume and consume and consume, and the end result is nothing more than a stinking pile of wasted life.

The world we live in convinces us that this is okay, but it isn't. God created us for so much more than consuming. He invites us to be investors in His eternal kingdom. We are invited to be adopted children into His family and to share in the family business. God is in the seeking-and-saving-the-lost business. His industry is growing heaven.

The Church is Christ's physical presence on earth. We are here to fulfill His mission. Jesus gave His life to save the world. He told His disciples that they must lay down their lives in order to follow Him. Christians are followers of Jesus. Followers of Jesus do what Jesus did. Jesus gave His life to build eternity. If we are truly His followers, we should expect to give our lives as well.

It is crucial to understand that we are not merely recipients of God's kingdom—we are participants in building God's kingdom. We are called by God to invest in eternity and the best thing about this particular investment is the promised return. God takes what we give Him and multiplies it to grow His kingdom.

When we use resources for His glory, the end result is more people in the kingdom of heaven.

Jesus is looking for investors who understand what it means to be His disciples. He gives to us and then expects us to use resources appropriately. This is no small matter, and Jesus was crystal clear on His expectations.

> "Again, it will be like a man going on a journey, who called his servants and entrusted his wealth to them. To one he gave five bags of gold, to another two bags, and to another one bag, each according to his ability. Then he went on his journey. The man who had received five bags of gold went at once and put his money to work and gained five bags more. So also, the one with two bags of gold gained two more. But the man who had received one bag went off, dug a hole in the ground and hid his master's money.
>
> "After a long time the master of those servants returned and settled accounts with them. The man who had received five bags of gold brought the other five. 'Master,' he said, 'you entrusted me with five bags of gold. See, I have gained five more.'
>
> "His master replied, 'Well done, good and faithful servant! You have been faithful

with a few things; I will put you in charge of many things. Come and share your master's happiness!'

"The man with two bags of gold also came. 'Master,' he said, 'you entrusted me with two bags of gold; see, I have gained two more.'

"His master replied, 'Well done, good and faithful servant! You have been faithful with a few things; I will put you in charge of many things. Come and share your master's happiness!'

"Then the man who had received one bag of gold came. 'Master,' he said, 'I knew that you are a hard man, harvesting where you have not sown and gathering where you have not scattered seed. So I was afraid and went out and hid your gold in the ground. See, here is what belongs to you.'

"His master replied, 'You wicked, lazy servant! So you knew that I harvest where I have not sown and gather where I have not scattered seed? Well then, you should have put my money on deposit with the bankers, so that when I returned I would have received it back with interest.

"'So take the bag of gold from him and give it to the one who has ten bags. For whoever has will be given more, and they will have an abundance. Whoever does not have, even

what they have will be taken from them. And
throw that worthless servant outside, into the
darkness, where there will be weeping and
gnashing of teeth.'"

Matthew 25:14-30

Jesus is our Master and He has gone on a journey to prepare our heavenly home. He will return and ask us to give an account for how we lived. He entrusts life to us, not to consume but to invest. We are not merely to meander through life waiting to die. We are called to invest ourselves into the kingdom-building mission of Jesus. Multiplication is expected. We are not called by God to simply preserve our saved, little lives. We are called to invest aggressively in eternity. He expects us to get to work and multiply.

Financial giving is one important way to do this. For many, it is an entry point into purposeful, exponential, kingdom-building living. Give and the heart follows. Give and other spiritual disciplines will likely develop. Give and the cultural idol of money is rendered impotent. Give and confidence in the lordship of Jesus increases greatly. Give and heaven multiplies.

God expects you to use every resource at your disposal to advance His mission. Nothing is to be held back. Nothing is off limits. Whether you have a little or a lot is not the issue. The issue is whether or not what you have is purposefully put to work to build God's kingdom.

You have two options. Bury or invest?

The fearful servant buried his master's money. He wasted it by not putting it to work. The master called the servant wicked and lazy. The most wicked thing a Christian can do is refuse to invest in eternity. Buried treasure is wasted treasure. We bury our treasure when we refuse to give, when we squander resources on empty pleasures, when we hoard money out of fear, and when we deny the reality that God cares about how we use money.

The faithful servants invested their master's money. They put it to work and the money doubled. God expects us to multiply. Life on this earth has eternal consequences. Faithful servants of God understand this and aggressively invest in eternity.

Everyone is in one of three conditions… dead, dying, or multiplying.

The dead are lost. They do not know Christ. They have not received eternal life. Their sin hangs over them as a shroud of death. There is no hope for eternity, only the despair of today. Their greatest treasure—life—is buried in the ground because death is all they know.

"For the wages of sin is death, but the gift of God is eternal life in Christ Jesus our Lord."
Romans 6:23

The dying know the salvation of Jesus but neglect His power for living. They squander life by merely waiting around for death. They continue to conform to the patterns of this world and are exhausted and confused by their duplicity. There is no joy, hope, or purpose. Fear dominates the dying and they become consumed with digging holes. Since they have not fully taken hold of eternal life, they cling to today. Worry and dread drown out hope, and they revert to their former way of living.

"But mark this: There will be terrible times in the last days. People will be lovers of themselves, lovers of money, boastful, proud, abusive, disobedient to their parents, ungrateful, unholy, without love, unforgiving, slanderous, without self-control, brutal, not lovers of the

good, treacherous, rash, conceited, lovers of
pleasure rather than lovers of God— having a
form of godliness but denying its power. Have
nothing to do with such people."
2 Timothy 3:1-5

Many have a form of godliness but deny its power. People in this condition are like the living dead. They have received eternal life but choose to remain in death. Zombie-Christians are creepy-Christians. The worries of this world choke the life of Jesus right out of them. They find themselves in a loveless, joyless relationship with Jesus. They go through the motions, following the pattern of this world, hanging on for death with a slim hope that heaven just might be real and that they might squeak in by the skin of their teeth.

The multiplying are alive with passion and purpose. They thrust themselves headlong into building God's eternal portfolio. They understand the promised return of their investment and gleefully give with the anticipation of there being more people in the kingdom of heaven. They comprehend that today's investment resounds eternally. They possess authentic hope that is demonstrated through generous giving.

"Still other seed fell on good soil, where it produced a crop—a hundred, sixty or thirty times what was sown. Whoever has ears, let them hear."

Matthew 13:8-9

Good soil produces good crops. Good crops are ones that multiply. Consider what your life is producing. Are you producing an exponential gain for Jesus, or is your treasure so buried in the here and now that only death looms on the horizon?

This is a simple matter. When you give, heaven grows. You can fight it, argue about it, and try to reason it away, but there is no denying that giving matters. Ultimately there are only two questions to consider. Will you invest in eternity, and if so, how much?

"Remember this: Whoever sows sparingly will also reap sparingly, and whoever sows generously will also reap generously. Each of you should give what you have decided in your heart to give, not reluctantly or under compulsion, for God loves a cheerful giver. And God is able to bless you abundantly, so

that in all things at all times, having all that you need, you will abound in every good work."
2 Corinthians 9:6-8

Big harvests come from sowing generously. Ask God what percentage of your income is generous. Decide to give. Make a plan and give cheerfully with confidence that Jesus will multiply your generosity. God is able to give you everything you need in order to do everything He calls you to do. You will lack nothing required for life when you trust Jesus in this.

Icing on the Cake

B irthday parties are great.

One of the best things about a birthday party is that the day is not about you. It is fun to celebrate a family member or friend's special day. We make most days about us. We think in terms of self and orchestrate events to play out in our best interests, but a good birthday party is a wonderful escape from egocentric living.

I have asked people what they think the best part of a birthday party is, and far and away the most common response has been cake and ice cream. At first glance, that answer does have merit. Cake and ice cream are wonderful. They are a delicious combination that makes any day better. It is also the part of the birthday party where attendees consume. Since we tend to think from the vantage point of consumers, it stands to reason that cake and ice cream would be our favorite part of the birthday party experience.

I am just not buying it.

Having attended a number of birthday parties over the years, I have observed the polarizing nature of cake and ice cream. No matter what is served, not everyone is happy. There are always detractors. Some people think that you can only serve vanilla ice cream with chocolate cake or vice versa. Others are purists and do not believe in the mixing of the flavors. They want vanilla on vanilla or chocolate on chocolate. There are progressive types who believe in options. They think there should be a variety of flavors and combinations to choose from. Others, who are quite frankly wrong, believe that cake and ice cream should be served separately. How those people get invited to birthday parties is beyond me.

My point is that cake and ice cream is the one part of a birthday party that is sure to disappoint. We carry expectations about what we hope to consume, and if those expectations are not met, we are disappointed. We are disappointed when we do not get the piece of cake we wanted…the corner piece, the piece with not-too-much icing, the biggest piece, the piece with letter "A," and so forth. We get disappointed with the ice cream…the scoop wasn't big enough, they didn't serve it fast enough and it started to melt, they served it on top of the cake instead of beside the cake, and so on. If you get a fork, you wish you had a spoon and you wonder why they didn't splurge for sporks.

We make cake and ice cream about our preferences and what we can consume. Selfishness leads to misery. Cake and ice cream is not the best part of a birthday party. The best part of a birthday party is watching the birthday boy or girl open gifts.

We love to give gifts. It is in our DNA. Just watch kids at a birthday party and you will witness this truth in action. Kid's faces light up when the birthday boy or girl grabs their package off of the table and starts to unwrap it. There is great anticipation and joy on the face of the gift-giver. It is the best part of the birthday party.

This phenomenon should not be all that surprising. After all, we are created in the image of God, and God loves to give good gifts to His children. He lavishes us with love and fills us with the gift of His Holy Spirit. If you are a Christian, then you have a new identity. You are being transformed. God is changing you from consumer to giver.

"In everything I did, I showed you that by this kind of hard work we must help the weak, remembering the words the Lord Jesus himself said: 'It is more blessed to give than to receive.'"

Acts 20:35

Giving is where it is at. Giving is the icing on the cake! There comes a point when you realize that every day is the Lord's Day. There is an "aha moment" when you understand that life is all about Him. He invites us to His party, and the best part is giving Him the only gift He desires. God wants you. He wants all of you, not a portion or a part, but all of you.

Are you holding anything back? Will you pray and ask God what percentage of your income is generous? Will you listen to His answer and make a plan to give? Will you trust God and give?

If you do, you will find that giving is the best part of God's party. It is indeed the icing on His cake.

About the Author

Bo Chancey is the senior pastor of Manchester Christian Church in Manchester, New Hampshire. Bo is a gifted communicator who is passionate about challenging people to fall madly in love with Jesus Christ. He believes that church should be fun and that God desperately desires all people to find the freedom of living an abundant life in Him.

Bo received a degree in History and Speech Communications at Texas A&M University. He and his wife, Somer have three children: Alizah, Aysen and Ensley. Bo enjoys sports, writing songs, spending time with his family and preaching.

bochancey.com

facebook.com/bochancey

twitter.com/bochancey